Rubbish

Written by Charlotte Raby
Illustrated by Ángeles Peinador

Collins

a red digger

a rear loader for the rubbish

a red digger

a rear loader for the rubbish

a long ladder

a power tool

a long ladder

a power tool

a chair with a missing leg

a tower

a chair with a missing leg

a tower

🐾 Review: After reading 🐾

Use your assessment from hearing the children read to choose any GPCs, words or tricky words that need additional practice.

Read 1: Decoding

- Turn to pages 2 and 3. Draw the children's attention to the word **digger**. Can they find any other words with the GPC "er"? (*loader*)
- Turn to pages 6 and 7. Ask the children to find and read the word with the sound /ow/. (*power*)

Read 2: Vocabulary

- Go back through the book and discuss the pictures. Encourage children to talk about details that stand out for them. Use a dialogic talk model to expand on their ideas and recast them in full sentences, as naturally as possible.
- Work together to expand vocabulary by naming objects in the pictures that children do not know.
- Ask children to point to and read the word that answers these questions:
  - Page 2 – What machine is the woman driving? (*digger*)
  - Page 12 – What piece of furniture is at the rubbish tip? (*chair*)

Read 3: Comprehension

- What are the people doing behind the rubbish collectors, on pages 6 and 7? (*working on a building site*)
- Turn to pages 14 and 15 and ask: Can you tell me what happens at each stage?